# MY VOICE WILL GO ON

First published in 2026 by OH
An Imprint of HEADLINE PUBLISHING GROUP LIMITED

1

**Disclaimer:**
This book has not been licensed, approved, sponsored, or endorsed by Céline Dion.

Céline Dion is a registered trademark owned by Feeling Productions Inc, 2540 Daniel-Johnson Boulevard, Bureau 755, Laval, Québec, H7T 2S3, Canada.



Cataloguing in Publication Data is available from the British Library

ISBN 978-1-03543-653-8

Compiled and written by Malcolm Croft
Editorial: Victoria Denne
Designed and typeset in Avenir by Andy Jones
Project manager: Russell Porter
Production: Arlene Lestrade
Printed and bound in Dubai

MIX
Paper | Supporting responsible forestry
FSC® C104740

Headline's policy is to use papers that are natural, renewable and recyclable products and made from wood grown in well-managed forests and other controlled sources. The logging and manufacturing processes are expected to conform to the environmental regulations of the country of origin.

HEADLINE PUBLISHING GROUP LIMITED
An Hachette UK Company
Carmelite House, 50 Victoria Embankment, London EC4Y 0DZ

The authorised representative in the EEA is Hachette Ireland, 8 Castlecourt Centre, Dublin 15, D15 XTP3, Ireland (email: info@hbgi.ie)

www.headline.co.uk www.hachette.co.uk

# MY VOICE WILL GO ON

## THE LITTLE GUIDE TO CÉLINE DION

UNOFFICIAL AND UNAUTHORIZED

OH

# CONTENTS

# INTRODUCTION

Céline Dion, often hailed as the Queen of Power Ballads, is one of the world's most beloved singers, holding the record as the bestselling Canadian and French-language recording artist of all time. With over 245 million records sold, she is one of the biggest-selling female recording artists in music history. Since her teenage years, Céline has been a global phenomenon, first achieving superstardom in her native Canada, then expanding her reach to Europe and, ultimately, the world. Her voice has touched us all.

Under the guidance of her manager-husband and guardian angel, René Angélil, Céline has demonstrated her enduring power repeatedly. Her career is marked by a series of monumental achievements, from her debut album at age 12 to her Eurovision win in 1988, followed by double Grammy and Academy Award wins for the iconic film themes "Beauty and the Beast" and "My Heart Will Go On". There's also the 20 multi-million-selling albums, a successful fragrance line, and two – yes, two! – groundbreaking Las Vegas residencies. These residencies achieved what no other artist had done before: they redefined Las Vegas as the world's premier entertainment capital.

Despite facing significant personal tragedies, including René's passing in 2016 and her debilitating battle with Stiff Person Syndrome, Céline is experiencing a divine resurgence, or Célinaissance, as we've coined it, in her fifties. Her 2024 documentary *I Am: Céline Dion* has brought a renewed spotlight to her music and business empire, making her relevant – and cool – to a whole new generation. She's even best friends with Deadpool. What she does next is anyone's guess!

This tiny tome you hold in your hands is a collection of Céline's incredible quotes, offering a deep dive into her elegant wit and wisdom, and the wonder of her extraordinary life. From her very first interview in 1981 all the way up to today; its a treasure trove filled with as many hilarious anecdotes, inspiring life mottos and essential trivia as she has pairs of designer shoes. Well, almost.

Welcome to Team Céline.

Enjoy!

# CHAPTER ONE

# LA PETITE QUÉBÉCOISE

Céline's extraordinary talent was undeniable from a young age.

She sang on kitchen table tops at two, weddings at five, released her debut album when she was 12 and won Eurovision at 20.

Let's discover her beauty and her life beats all over again...

# MARCH 30,1968

The day Thérèse Tanguay and Adhémar Dion welcomed Céline Dion, the youngest of 14 children, in Charlemagne, Quebec.

The No.1 song in Canada at the time was "The Ballad of Bonnie and Clyde" by Georgie Fame.

“I’d say: ‘Hang in there, everything will work out just fine.’”

Céline, when asked “What would you say to the young Céline who was bullied at school?”, interview with Alix Girod, *Elle*, May 24, 2019

“

I started to sing when I was five years old. One night I told my mother, ‘Please let me sing’. And she said, ‘Oh god not another one!’

”

Céline, on her parents learning that she wanted to be an singer (in a family full of musicians), interview with *Entertainment Tonight*, 1990

“I have 13 brothers and sisters and they are all singers, they all play instruments. My parents used to tour with members of my family. So they are artists themselves – everybody in my family wanted to be in show business.”

Céline, on her musical family, upbringing and parents, interview with Ralph Benmergui, CBC, February 1993

# April 30, 1988

The day that Céline won the Eurovision Song Contest, representing Switzerland with the song "Ne Partez Pas Sans Moi" ("Don't Leave Without Me").

Age 20, Céline won the contest by just one point – the closest margin in the contest's history! – beating the United Kingdom's entry, "Go", performed by Scott Fitzgerald.

“

I received a call when I was in Montreal where I live. I was asked to go to Ireland to represent Switzerland... as a French Canadian Québécoise... for the Eurovision Song Contest. I didn't understand! 'What about people in Switzerland?', I thought! 'What are they going to think? Where's she coming from? We don't even know her!'

”

Céline, on her Eurovision Song Contest selection process in 1988, interview with Jonathan Ross, *The Jonathan Ross Show*, November 9, 2013

“

I was brought up with true family values. There is an incredible richness to family. It gives you tools to be able to face the extraordinary moments, the harder times, the ups and downs

”

Céline, on the importance of family, interview with Laurent Boyer, *Fréquenstar*, July 30, 1998

"

When I was 12, René asked me to sing in front of him. He had received, some weeks before, a tape with a demo of the song that my mother had written for me. René took some time to listen to it. My brother then gave him a call and told him, 'Mr. Angélil, I know you haven't listened to the tape because you would've phoned right away!' René then said, 'I'm gonna listen to it, I'll call you right back.' After he listened to it, he called back saying he was very interested in meeting me.

"

Céline, on how she came to meet René Angélil, her future manager (and husband), interview with Laurent Boyer, *Fréquenstar*, July 30, 1998

“I had always lived surrounded by adults and children a lot older than me. I learned everything I needed to know from them. As far as I was concerned, real life existed around them.”

Céline, on age, in relation to her 27-year age gap with René Angélil, *Céline Dion: My Story, My Dream*, December 4, 2001

“

The way that I grew up was the most fabulous way to grow up with love, attention and affection.

”

Céline Dion, on her cherished upbringing, interview with Ralph Benmergui, CBC, February 1993

Famed for more than 30 years as the "Queen of Power Ballads", Céline has released 27 studio albums, seven live albums, 20 compilation albums, and 25 box sets since 1981.

Today, she has sold more than 245 million albums, making her the seventh bestselling female solo artist of all time, behind only Madonna, Rihanna, Mariah, Whitney, Taylor and Beyoncé.

“I dropped out of school because it was taking me away from music, from my happiness, from my dreams.”

Céline, on leaving school at age 15 to pursue her music dreams, interview with Charles P. Alexander, *Time,* March 7, 1994

# June 11, 1981

The day Céline released her debut single, "Ce N'était Qu'un Rêve" ("It Was Only a Dream").

The lyrics were written by her mother, Thérèse, and her brother Jacques composed the music. It spent six weeks on the charts in Quebec, peaking at No.8.

> “While I was singing, René started to cry. I knew then I had done a good job.”

Céline, on her first audition with René Angélil when she was 12 (he was 38), interview with Diana Pearl, *People,* June 19, 2025

"At 17 years old, my feelings started to change for René. I kind of saw him differently. I have to say that for my mom he was not... the ideal prince charming."

Céline, on her changing feelings towards René Angélil and her mom's reaction, interview with Erin O'Sullivan, *Access Hollywood*, September 12, 2013

"She [Céline's mom] tried everything to kill him and make me snap out of it... [But] my love for him was so strong that my whole family was in love with him and she had no choice. Love won."

Céline, on the power of love, seen in article by Jason MacNeil, Huffington Post, September 12, 2013

“

My private life is my career.

”

Céline, on sharing her life with her fans throughout her career, interview with Laurent Boyer, *Fréquenstar,* July 30, 1998

# September 11, 1984

The day 16-year-old Céline performed for Pope John Paul II and 65,000 people at Montreal's Olympic Stadium in Canada. It was her first official live performance – and her biggest!

During his papal visit, Céline sang "Une Colombe" ("A Dove"); it was a beautiful performance that showcased the powerful potential of her singing voice.

"I am not an Anglophone artist and the public understands that. Everywhere I go in the world, I say that I'm proud to be Québécoise."

Céline, on – controversially – refusing to accept awards as an "Anglophone artist" at the start of her career, interview with Brendan Kelly, *Montreal Gazette,* June 1991

Céline is named after the 1966 song “Céline” by French singer Hugues Aufray.

The song tells the tragic story of an old blind man and a little girl named Céline.

The name “Céline” is of French and Latin origin. It is a derivative of the name “Caelina” and means “Heaven”.

“I’m not a minor. This is a free country. No one has the right to prevent me from loving whoever I want to.”

Céline, on her controversial age-gap relationship with René Angélil, 27 years her senior, *Céline Dion: My Story, My Dream*, December 4, 2001

"

I was lucky to have parents who were willing to help me open this book of dreams and give me the tools to help me fulfil my dream. My parents didn't go to school, but at the same time, they have all the talents in the world. Very generous people, they've raised 14 children with nothing… but with everything at the same time.

"

Céline, on her love and respect for her parents and her family, interview with Laurent Boyer, *Fréquenstar*, July 30, 1998

# *La Voix Du Bon Dieu*

At just 13 years old, Céline released her debut album, *La Voix du Bon Dieu* (*The Voice of God*), in 1981.

The album's success quickly established her as a national star in Quebec, Canada. The album was financed by René Angélil, Céline's manager (and later husband). He mortgaged his home to start his own record company just to fund it.

Her second LP, a Christmas album, *Céline Dion Chante Noël*, was released a month later!

“

Music is for me an international language. It’s a dream come true to hear my songs on American radio because while I was recording my debut album in Canada I was telling myself that ‘This is my first recording, it doesn’t mean that it’s going to work.’

”

Céline, on recording her debut album (aged 12), and her early aspirations for stardom, interview with Mary Hart, *Entertainment Tonight*, April, 1990

“

When I look at myself in the past, I get very emotional. I was not pretty, I had teeth problems, and I was very skinny. I didn’t fit the mold.

”

Céline, on having been bullied at school and lacking confidence in her early years in the business due to her appearance, interview with Nandini D’Souza, *W Magazine*, October 1, 2007

"

I didn't expect to reach No.4 on the *Billboard* with 'Where Does My Heart Beat Now'. It's a first experience for me, in English. It was a great surprise, because I didn't expect that at all. I think everyone dreams of being famous in the USA and to go as far as possible! I can't believe it yet, on the *Billboard*. It's a beautiful dream and I hope it will continue.

"

Céline, on her first taste of success in the US, interview with Laurent Boyer, *Fréquenstar*, July 30, 1998

"At Eurovision, I looked like a horse and I felt like a horse. Let me elaborate on that… You can bet on the artist that you want the country to win. So my husband, René Angélil, who is a gambler, bet on me. *A lot of money*. And I felt like I was a horse that really needed to win the race."

Céline, on her 1988 Eurovision Song Contest win, interview with Jonathan Ross, *The Jonathan Ross Show*, November 9, 2013

“

# My big dream is to become an international star.

”

Céline, on her aspirations in her first French TV interview, interview with Michel Drucker, January 29, 1983

# CHAPTER TWO

# VOICE OF GOD

An influence to her peers, an inspiration to a younger generation of artists and an icon to her millions of fans, Céline Dion is without a doubt a once-in-a-lifetime voice of a generation.

And what a voice it is…

"I was at the beginning of my career. 'Beauty and the Beast' is the song that gave me a name in a way. My songs were being played on the radio but people did not know who sings that song... When the song was offered to me it put me on the map. It gave me a name."

Céline, on "Beauty and the Beast", her award-winning song from Disney's 1991 *Beauty and the Beast*, interview with *Entertainment Tonight*, January 10, 2012

# August 13, 1973

The day that, at the age of five, Céline made her public singing debut at her brother Michel's wedding.

She stood on a table and sang Christine Charbonneau's 1972 hit, "Du Fil, Des Aiguilles Et Du Coton" ("Thread, Needles and Cotton").

Céline Dion has won a total of five Grammy Awards from 16 nominations:

1. **Best Pop Performance by a Duo/Group with Vocals** for "Beauty and the Beast" (1993)
2. **Album of the Year** for *Falling into You* (1997)
3. **Best Pop Album** for *Falling into You* (1997)
4. **Record of the Year** for "My Heart Will Go On" (1999)
5. **Best Female Pop Vocal** Performance for "My Heart Will Go On" (1999)

**"I don't want to dream the impossible dream but, one day, I would like to win a Grammy. I'm very confident in myself. I'd love to have a career like Barbra Streisand or Whitney Houston. I want to see the world."**

Céline, on her dream of winning a Grammy Award, interview with Brendan Kelly, *Montreal Gazette*, J une 1991

"I don't have an eating problem, and there's nothing more I can say about it. My work requires me to be in great physical shape. I wouldn't have been able to give up to 100 shows a year and travel ceaselessly from one end of the world to the other if I had eaten too much or not enough, or if, as certain magazines have claimed, I made myself throw up after each meal."

Céline, on the constant tabloid and media rumours about her body weight, *Céline Dion: My Story, My Dream*, December 4, 2001

“Switzerland, we won! And they loved me after. They gave me a lot of chocolate.”

Céline, on her Eurovision Song Contest win for Switzerland endearing her to the nation, interview with Jonathan Ross, *The Jonathan Ross Show*, November 9, 2013

# December 17, 1994

The day 26-year-old Céline Dion married her manager, René Angélil, at a lavish ceremony at Notre-Dame Basilica, Montreal, Canada.

The extravagant event was televised, with Céline famously wearing a 7 lb headpiece adorned with 2,000 Swarovski diamonds!

She later described the magical ceremony as "the ceremony of my dreams".

"

I grew up in a very, very, very small house. My mum was brilliant enough to put a pillow in a drawer for a baby to sleep in. We were safe and warm and taken care of. Three or four of us in the same bed was normal to us. We weren't poor, but we never had money. We were given love and affection and support. What else did we need?

"

Céline, on growing up with 13 siblings with little money, interview by Tim Shaeffer, *Vanity Fair*, December 14, 2011

Céline has amassed more than 6.5 billion streams on Spotify.

Her most popular track is "My Heart Will Go On", the love theme from *Titanic*, with more than 650 million streams.

"I started performing when I was five. I am a singer. I sing in English, in French, I've sung in Mandarin, I've sung in Japanese, in Spanish and in Italian and people have come, they've always come. That, for me, was the proof that I was, and that I am, truly a singer. One thing's for sure, I'll love that feeling until the day I die."

Céline, on her love of singing and being a singer, interview with Clovis Goux, *Vogue*, April 22, 2024

“My favourite game as a child was to sing.”

Céline, on her love of singing as a child, interview with Charles P. Alexander, *Time*, March 7, 1994

# "René always says he discovered me but it was I who discovered him!"

Céline, on her manager and husband René Angélil, interview with Laurent Boyer, *Fréquenstar,* July 30, 1998

> That filled so many unexplained, emotional holes from my childhood – especially during my school years. I don't want to say I have scars, but when I sing it live, it is for many people like me, who have suffered so much because they felt awkward and unwanted when they were younger.

Céline, on the power of the song "At Seventeen" and her own teenage years, interview with Elio Iannacci, *Maclean's*, October 27, 2013

"Do I have any regrets? I don't know – and I don't care. The stage, my family, my children and my songs have taught me everything I know. When I was younger, there was no school, I had no friends. I had the stage and my family. I didn't want anything else."

Céline, on regrets on becoming a star so young, interview with Clovis Goux, *Vogue France*, April 22, 2024

“He asked me: ‘Can you sing a little bit of the song for me?’ Singing in front of just one person is worse than performing for a crowd of 20,000. He gave me a pencil and said: ‘Imagine this is a microphone.’ He wanted to make sure that it was really me singing on the demo. While I was singing, he started crying. That’s how I met René.”

Céline, on her first audition for René, aged 12, interview with Clovis Goux, *Vogue France*, April 22, 2024.

# “Some people do drugs. I buy shoes. I have about 3,000 pairs!”

Céline, on her obsession with fashion – and designer shoes, interview with Tim Shaeffer, *Vanity Fair*, December 14, 2011

“René had become the object of the love that I sang about, he was the man of my songs… I wanted only one man for my entire life. I knew that one day it would be René.”

Céline, on her 30-year relationship with René,
*Céline Dion: My Story, My Dream*, December 4, 2001

# January 14, 2016

The day René Angélil passed away, at the age of 73, after a long battle with throat cancer. He died at his home in Las Vegas, just two days before his 74th birthday.

His death was a profound loss for Céline, who had been his caregiver for years.

In a tragic turn of events, her beloved brother Daniel also died from cancer just two days later.

"I have 13 siblings, and I was the last. I wore all their clothes. My mom didn't have money to buy it, so she made the clothes."

Céline, on her siblings and her upbringing, interview with Nathalie Atkinson, *The Globe and Mail*, October 9, 2019

“

I love every single item in my wardrobe, because each one is linked to a specific time in my life.

”

Céline, on her love (and hoarding) of clothes, interview with Alix Girod, *Elle*, May 24, 2019

“

My inner voice is a lot stronger than my singing voice.

”

Céline, on her confidence in who she is,
interview with Oprah Winfrey, *The Oprah Winfrey Show*,
November 13, 2007

“

I was in a suite with a piano at Caesars Palace. James Horner started to play the song. With all the respect that I have for James, he is not the greatest singer. René stopped him: 'James, James, listen to me. You're not doing justice to the song right now. Let's just have Céline make a demo.'
I wanted to choke my husband. Because I didn't want to do it!

”

Céline, on first hearing "My Heart Will Go On" – and not wanting to sing the song at all, interview with Mickey Rapkin, *Billboard*, May 18, 2017

“

I got my wings from my mom. Every single day I told my mom, ‘Mom, I want to sing; I want to become a singer. I want to be in show business,’ and my mom always said to me, ‘Céline, I want you to sing, but professionally with your own songs.’

”

Céline, on her mother’s influence on her early career, interview with Oprah Winfrey, *The Oprah Winfrey Show*, March 21, 1997

"I have an extraordinary life and people are jealous."

Céline, on her success and stardom – and toxic critics who judge her every move, interview with Chrissy Iley, *The Guardian*, December 10, 2007

“It’s wonderful to be wanted and to be loved.”

Céline, on her immense success, interview with Larry King, CNN *Larry King Live*, December 22, 2010

“

Life doesn’t give you any answers. You just have to live it! I have this illness for some unknown reason. The way I see it, I have two choices. Either I train like an athlete and work super hard, or I switch off and it’s over, I stay at home, listen to my songs, stand in front of my mirror and sing to myself. I’ve chosen to work with all my body and soul, from head to toe, with a medical team. I want to be the best I can be. My goal is to see the Eiffel Tower again!

”

Céline, on Stiff Person Syndrome (SPS), interview with Clovis Goux, *Vogue France*, April 22, 2024

> “I’ve had a thirty-year career as me. I’m not going to reinvent myself.”

Céline, on not feeling the need to reinvent herself in her fifties, interview with Sergio Kletnoy, *Cosmopolitan*, November 1, 2013

“

I said, ‘OK, well, I’m glad that you liked the demo.’ James Horner then said, ‘We might not have to do it again.’ I said, ‘What are you talking about?’

”

Céline, on her first demo vocal being the final vocal performance on the hit song "My Heart Will Go On", interview with Mickey Rapkin, *Billboard*, May 18, 2017

# CHAPTER THREE

# DREAM CAME TRUE

Céline's dream of a life less ordinary came true when she met René Angélil, a Quebec-based music manager who bet big on Céline's singing skills.

More than just music industry history, they made each other's dreams come true...

“I’m not saying that I don’t care what people think of me, but I’ve reached a point in my life where I can let myself make my own decisions and choices.”

Céline, on no longer listening to her critics, interview with Katie Connor, *Elle*, May 1, 2019

"

My son is 12 and he could not believe that Sia wrote me a song. He thought it was a mistake because I'm not cool. I'm a mother, she is going to write for Rihanna, not for me.

"

Céline, on "Loved Me Back to Life" (written by pop superstar Sia), interview with Sergio Kletnoy, *Cosmopolitan*, November 1, 2013

> "For me, being cool is to feel happy and stable and sure of myself."

Céline, on what it means to be "cool"', interview with Chrissy Iley, *The Guardian*, December 10, 2007

> "When I see a rainbow, a sunset, a beautiful dance number, I laugh, I cry. I'm in love."

Céline, on still finding love in life despite the passing of her husband, René, interview with Catherine Thorbecke and Faryn Shiro, *Good Morning America*, April 2, 2019

"

That would be in 'All By Myself' – it's still hard to sing today. I was in Montreal and producer David [Foster] was in Malibu and called me to ask me if I could [attempt] the song in my register so I sang it to him over the phone and he was happy…

When I get to Malibu to record the song he tells me he's rearranged it three notes higher. He said, and I'll never forget it, 'Don't worry if you can't sing it, Whitney Houston is in the studio next door.' That gave me the pipes that I needed. ”

Céline, on the hardest note she's ever had to hit, interview with Elio Iannacci, *Maclean's*, October 27, 2013

"When I hit that note, what you hear in the back is not the drums, it's my clothes that exploded! I think everything exploded, my pants, my bra, my shirt. People stop breathing when I hit that note."

Céline, on that note in "All By Myself", interview with Tom Power, *CBC Radio*, September 20, 2019

* The long and famous high note leading into the key change – an F5, FYI

“It probably sounds very strange to say this to you, but when I was diagnosed [with Stiff Person Syndrome], I was happy. I was finally able to move with the wave, not against it.”

Céline, on her SPS diagnosis in 2022, interview with Liam Hess, *Vogue*, May 23, 2024.

"James Cameron [director of 1997's *Titanic*] didn't want to have a song in his movie. 'My movie is big enough, I don't need something bigger, I don't need any singer,' he said. And I don't blame him. But [composer] James Horner told him: 'I'm not going to tell you who sang the song. Just please give me a favour and listen just one time.'"

Céline, on how "My Heart Will Go On" became the love theme for *Titanic*, interview with Mickey Rapkin, *Billboard*, May 18, 2017

> “When your voice brings you joy… you’re the best of yourself.”

Céline, on her voice – and the happiness it creates for herself and others, documentary interview with Irene Taylor, *I Am: Céline Dion*, 2024, directed by Irene Taylor

"Imagine facing life and death in one day."

Céline, on René being declared in remission from skin cancer on the same day she discovered she was pregnant with twin boys, interview with Chrissy Iley, *Women's Weekly*, August 14, 2024

“René was the first and only – unless you count the kiss I gave somebody* else on the porch of my sister’s house.”

Céline, on her first kiss, interview by Tim Shaeffer, Vanity Fair, December 14, 2011

* His name was Sylvian, FYI

“

I’ve toured the world, I’ve done amazing things. I’m very proud of my career, and especially the fact that I knew how to stay true to the same person, with the same values… Because of course I could’ve gone off my head many times. It’s easy. Everything’s possible in this job.

”

Céline, on never having gone off the rails despite the immense pressures of fame, interview with Marie-France Bazzo, Radio Canada, September 6, 2004

“I had a $200 million-dollar necklace around my neck. I had six bodyguards on the red carpet. I thought it was for me, but it was not for me. It was for the necklace.”

Céline, on her legendary Academy Award ceremony performance of "My Heart Will Go On" in March 1997 and her iconic outfit, interview with Mickey Rapkin, *Billboard*, May 18, 2017

“

For me, fashion is art. When I put something on, I play. I don’t take myself seriously.

”

Céline, on her love of designer fashion, interview with Katie Connor, *Elle*, May 1, 2019

"

When people come to me and say, 'I want to be just like you; the only thing I want in life is to sing,' I tell them this: 'Please don't make your career your life.' Let it be your passion, let it bring you pleasure, but don't let it become your identity. You are so much more valuable than that.

"

Céline, on advice to aspiring singers, interview with Naomi Barr, *O (The Oprah Magazine)*, November 2007

“Today, I feel like a woman. I feel like a mother. I am a singer, a dreamer, before being Québécoise, American or French.”

Céline, on how she defines herself, interview with Clovis Goux, *Vogue France*, April 22, 2024

"Performing live is like making a high dive. I'm not scared to jump. The nerves come in the breath before you leap off the board."

Céline, on stage fright, interview by Tim Shaeffer, *Vanity Fair*, December 14, 2011

"If you want to be able to do the splits, you have to train your muscles to be flexible. Singing lessons is not singing, it's a workout."

Céline, on constantly training her voice to keep it fit for singing, interview with Clovis Goux, *Vogue France*, April 22, 2024

“

They told me, ‘You know that Kate Winslet said every time she hears ‘My Heart Will Go On’, she wants to throw up?’ And I answered, ‘Thank God she didn’t have to sing it!’.

”

Céline, on the overwhelming and over-played success of "My Heart Will Go On", interview with Mickey Rapkin, *Billboard*, May 18, 2017

“I was born to communicate on stage, with my team, and with my voice, and with my fans. It’s about sharing. I was born to do that. When I found myself on stage for the first time, in Quebec, I caught the bug! What has fame taken away from me? Nothing? Because I live every day, and I move forward.”

Céline, on celebrity and fame, interview with Clovis Goux, *Vogue France*, April 22, 2024

> “My fans bought me this house. They bought my records. But, you know, I don't just sing for free. It's my work. You're paid for what you do. And I work hard. But a lot of people work hard and they don't have anything. I was very fortunate, and people have bought my albums year after year, and they come to see the shows, and it's expensive, and they still come.”

Céline, on her $30 million mega-mansion home in Las Vegas, interview by Tim Shaeffer, *Vanity Fair*, December 14, 2011

> “When I was 15, my private life and my show business life were one. I gave myself. But now, at 30, I want a family life. I need to have intimate moments. And I need to see the difference between work and private life.”

Céline, on her work–life balance,* interview with Laurent Boyer, *Fréquenstar*, July 30, 1998

* On New Year's Day 2000, Céline announced a two-year hiatus from releasing music and live shows following the worldwide success of a string of hit singles.

René told me that talent is 20 per cent of success. Beyond that, you need good songs, the right timing, the right team. I had lots of doors to open, I had different ways of singing, but people gave me the keys to go to even more places.

Céline, on the ingredients required for sustainable success, interview with Clovis Goux, *Vogue France*, April 22, 2024.

“

It really shook me up. You hear a voice like that every 10, 20 years.

”

René Angélil, on first hearing Céline's voice, aged 12, interview with Larry King, CNN.com, October 22, 2002

"For over 30 years I've been in this industry because I've been trying too hard and I don't think there are many people around that are able to have this kind of longevity. To have a hit is one thing. To be disciplined enough to commit to a career is another. It is beyond talent. You can't pretend not to care."

Céline, on the reasons behind her enduring longevity and legacy in the music industry, interview with Elio Iannacci, *Maclean's*, October 27, 2013

“Singing in English can get flowery, it takes everything to impress, and I love that. Singing in French requires a lot of effort because you want to bring more subtlety.”

Céline, on the differences of singing and French and English, interview with Clovis Goux, *Vogue France*, April 22, 2024

“It’s maybe difficult for some people to believe that even though I do have an extraordinary life, I am a normal person.”

Céline, on staying down-to-earth, interview by Tim Shaeffer, *Vanity Fair*, December 14, 2011

# CHAPTER FOUR

# ALL ABOARD TITANIQUE!

Despite being a multi-platinum Grammy-winning artist already, nobody on Earth could have predicted how much bigger Céline Dion would become with the 1997 release of *Titanic*'s love theme, "My Heart Will Go On".

It was an unsinkable song – unlike the Titanic, of course.

"I think I can do it. I think I'm all right. I think the kid is OK."

Céline, when asked if she knows she's a good singer, interview with Larry King, CNN, *Larry King Live*, November 22, 1999

# "I'm very comfortable in my skin… though it's peeling."

Céline, on her confidence on stage, performing at her world-famous Las Vegas show (and living in the desert!), interview with Nandini D'Souza, *W Magazine*, October 1, 2007

“

Beauty is you, it’s me, it’s what’s on the inside, it’s our dreams, it’s today.

”

Céline, on her definition of beauty, interview with Clovis Goux, *Vogue France*, April 22, 2024

“When I did the live show, even though there were a lot of butterflies, I did not want to cry. I love what I do and when I get embraced by the audience, I get taken by the emotions. So I said to myself, I want to have a good time, especially tonight, because it's my last show, so let's make it like a party!”

Céline, on her final show of her second Las Vegas residence in June 2019, interview with Tom Power, CBC Radio, September 20, 2019

After her diagnosis in 2022, Céline has been privately battling the rare neurological disorder known as Stiff Person Syndrome, which affects approximately one in a million people.

The condition, characterized by severe muscle spasms often triggered by noise, touch and stress, has also significantly impacted her ability to sing by affecting her vocal cords and her control over her voice.

"Every night in Vegas I'm like, 'Oh, gosh, I'm not going sing that song again.' And then that curtain opens and the smoke starts and people are crying. Every night when I start to sing that song... I'm so thankful that they did not listen to me."

Céline, on singing "My Heart Will Go On"every night – and for the 20,000th time – during her Las Vegas residences, interview with Mickey Rapkin, *Billboard*, May 18, 2017

“

I think talent is not enough. You need timing, hard work, and people around you.

”

Céline, on the ingredients needed to become successful in the music industry, interview with Ralph Benmergui, CBC, February 1993

"I never wanted to have just one hit, I wanted to have a career. So, when I was given a chance, I took it."

Céline, on taking the career chances when they came along, interview with Tom Power, CBC Radio, September 20, 2019

“

I always kind of thought that I can’t compete with Mariah and Whitney – but I can with myself. I can make myself better. And I always do so today.

”

Céline, on comparing herself to the other big singers of the 1990s, Mariah Carey and Whitney Houston, interview with Sergio Kletnoy, *Cosmopolitan*, November 1, 2013

"My dad didn't want to have any more children – but baby I'm worth it!"

Céline, on her father's decision to have no more children after their 13th – then Céline came along!, interview with Katie Connor, *Elle*, May 1, 2019

“

It’s difficult for a singer to perform five nights a week, it’s difficult for an artist to live in the desert – it’s difficult for a human being to live in the desert!

”

Céline, on moving to Las Vegas in 2003 for her "A New Day" residency at the Colosseum, interview with Marie-France Bazzo, Radio Canada, September 6, 2004

"I've sang 'My Heart Will Go On' about three gazillion times."

Céline, on "My Heart Will Go On", interview with Jimmy Fallon, *The Tonight Show Starring Jimmy Fallon*, July 21, 2016

"

I was very lucky, because I had 13 brothers and sisters, and I got everyone's hand-me-downs. When I got my first pay check, my first paid television appearances, I bought clothes for myself and dressed myself. With my first successes, I bought a house for myself and my husband, and for my parents and some family members too. After my first album in English, I was able to buy clothes by designers, and I started to read fashion magazines.

"

Céline, on how she became famous for being a "Queen of Fashion", interview with Clovis Goux, *Vogue France*, April 22, 2024

“I don’t know if the camera likes me, but I do like the camera.”

Céline, on her love of attention, interview with Nandini D’Souza, *W Magazine*, October 1, 2007

“I had to ring my mother to say, ‘I am not dead.’ I was freaking out. Imagine, my whole family were freaking out.”

Céline, on ridiculous tabloid rumours that circulated about Céline’s death from anorexia, interview with Chrissy Iley, *The Guardian*, December 10, 2007

"I was born in Quebec, my children were born in America. I have French blood, I have Québécoise blood and American blood. And wherever I go, I sing in a different language, I learn something, I steal a part of the culture that impresses me."

Céline, on her life and music transcending borders, interview with Clovis Goux, *Vogue France*, April 22, 2024

# “At 22, I had *legs*.”

Céline, on her famously long and slender legs, interview with Nathalie Atkinson, *The Globe and Mail*, October 9, 2019.

“

I can’t record ‘The Power of Love’ or ‘My Heart Will Go On’ again and again. I’m not Britney Spears but I do need to freshen up my sound – which I think we’ve done.

”

Céline, on the 2013 album Loved Me Back to Life, interview with Elio Iannacci, *Maclean’s*, October 27, 2013

# March 23, 1998

The date that director James Cameron's *Titanic* won 11 Academy Awards from 14 nominations, including Best Original Song for "My Heart Will Go On".

Presenter Madonna famously announced the win with a witty quip, reflecting the song's overwhelming popularity and expected victory: "What a shocker..."

* This was the night that Céline also became the first artist ever to perform two songs during the Oscars

"

In terms of music, I can try anything I want, even something that doesn't work at all, because I'm not putting my career in jeopardy. Ten or 15 years ago, I had to prove to myself that I could do it. I needed to prove to the industry and the people around me that I could do it, so I didn't take too many chances. Today is different. I feel like I can be edgier, because if it's too much, we can always do another album.

"

Céline, on being able to take risks now, interview with Nandini D'Souza, *W Magazine*, October 1, 2007

“

I had an image once about what is a man and what is a woman. The man is a tree. He's big, he's beautiful, moves the leaves, makes the shadow. We like to hug him. The roots of the tree is the woman. Without the roots he won't survive. We feed him to make him look good, preserve him. But it takes two together to make the tree healthy. The man can take the spotlight but only with the woman behind him. For me it's the tree of life.

”

Céline, on men and women, interview with Chrissy Iley, *The Guardian*, December 10, 2007

“

I feel like, let’s say there’s an apple tree, I’m an apple tree, and people are in line and I give them apples, the best, and I shine them, and they all leave with a basket of apples. And my branches are starting to fall sometimes, get crooked. And those branches are starting to produce a little less apples, but there’s still as many people in line. I don’t want them to wait in line if I don’t have apples for them.

”

Céline, on apple trees as a metaphor for the impact of her Stiff Person syndrome on her relationship with her fans, interview with Jayme Poisson, CBC News, June 13, 2024

“Thank you all! I love you right back. When I say that I'm happy to be here, I really mean it from my heart. Those who have been blessed enough to be here at the Grammy Awards must never take for granted the tremendous love and joy that music brings to our lives and to people all around the world.”

Céline, her heartfelt and emotional speech at the 2024 Grammy Awards while presenting the Album of the Year award,* which marked her first awards show appearance since her SPS diagnosis, February 5, 2024

* When she walked on stage, she was met with a long standing ovation

# “It’s a good problem to have.”

Céline, on having to sing the same hit songs overand over again during her phenomenal Las Vegas residencies, interview with Nandini D’Souza, *W Magazine*, October 1, 2007

“Show business can be a dangerous place. Anyone that goes in the jungle can see beauty, but you can be eaten up by nature as well. I protect myself.”

Céline, on the perils of fame and the music industry, interview with Janine Mackie, *Magniffisance*, 2022

“

When I had my son, I didn’t want to perform in Las Vegas anymore. I had a life for the first time. I knew then that I wanted to have more success as a mother than a singer. It was probably one of the hardest moments of my life.

”

Céline, on bringing her hit Las Vegas residency, "A New Day", to a close in 2007 for family reasons, interview with Oprah Winfrey, *The Oprah Winfrey Show*, November 13, 2007

“

When I recorded ‘My Heart Will Go On’, I didn’t think about a movie; I didn’t think about radio. I thought, ‘Sing the song, then get the heck out of there.

”

Céline, on recording the song "My Heart Will Go On", interview with Mickey Rapkin, *Billboard*, May 18, 2017

“

I’m very fortunate to have my husband – who’s 65 – not only because I love him, but because it would not work to have a husband my age who wants to go out twice a week. I would go crazy.

”

Céline, on not being a "party girl" and being grateful for her husband, interview with Nandini D'Souza, *W Magazine*, October 1, 2007

# CHAPTER FIVE

# CÉLINAISSANCE

For years, Céline Dion was dismissed by those who cared about being "cool".

However, her classic catalogue of hit songs has now been discovered by a new generation of fans.

This resurgence in popularity, affectionately dubbed a "Célinaissance" by us, has her star rising all over again.

"

My life started over at 50; I feel happy, I feel beautiful. I thought, 'I must have done something right for this to be happening.'

"

Céline, on turning 50, interview with Katie Connor, *Elle*, May 1, 2019

"If you want to go fast you go alone and if you want to go far you go together."

Céline, on her personal life philosophy, interview with Irene Taylor, *I Am: Céline Dion*, 2024, directed by Irene Taylor

> "The demands on women are too much. I would never start a career today because you have to have it all: you have to know how to sing, know how to dance and you have to look perfect. It's impossible."

Céline, on being thankful she is not starting her career in today's music industry, interview with Elio Iannacci, *Maclean's*, October 27, 2013

"It's me, who I am today. I grew. I didn't change. I evolved."

Céline, on 2007's Taking Chances, her first new album since the start of her gruelling Las Vegas residency for "A New Day", interview with Chrissy Iley, *The Guardian*, December 10, 2007

Céline has amassed nearly 6 billion views on YouTube! Here are her top ten most watched videos:

1. "I'm Alive" – *more than 615 million views!*
2. "That's the Way It Is"
3. "The Power of Love"
4. "A New Day Has Come"
5. "Pour que tu m'aimes encore"
6. "The Prayer"
7. "My Heart Will Go On"
8. "It's All Coming Back to Me Now"
9. "Ashes"
10. "Parler à mon père"

"When you have the soul of an artist, you can't live without it."

Céline, on being an artist, interview with Irene Taylor,
*I Am: Céline Dion*, 2024, directed by Irene Taylor

> **“**
>
> People thought we were absolutely bazooka for performing here!
>
> **”**

Céline, on first being told about the "crazy idea" of performing a residency in Las Vegas, interview with Katie Connor, *Elle*, May 1, 2019

Céline's groundbreaking "A New Day" residency, which ran from March 2003 to December 2007, redefined Las Vegas entertainment.

The show was held at the state-of-the-art Colosseum, a venue built specifically for Céline's residency. Over its five-year run, she performed an incredible 717 shows to almost 3 million fans.

The residency was a phenomenal success, becoming the highest-grossing of all time, with a total box-office take of more than $385 million – a record that may never be beat.

“

I haven’t beat the disease, as it’s still within me and always will be. I hope that we’ll find a miracle, a way to cure it with scientific research, but for now I have to learn to live with it. So that’s me, now with Stiff Person Syndrome. Five days a week I undergo athletic, physical and vocal therapy. I work on my toes, my knees, my calves, my fingers, my singing, my voice...

I have to learn to live with it now and stop questioning myself. At the beginning I would ask myself: why me? How did this happen? What have I done? Is this my fault?

Céline, on how she copes living with SPS, interview with Clovis Goux, *Vogue France*, April 22, 2024

> “I will be back on stage. Trust me, I will scream it out loud.”

Céline, on her aim to rediscover her voice so she can perform again, even with SPS, interview with Emma Vardy, *Sunday Times*, July 27, 2024

“We don’t come from Las Vegas, we don’t come from the United States, we come from Quebec – and we’re proud of it.”

Céline, on being proud of her Canadian roots, interview with Marie-France Bazzo, Radio Canada, September 6, 2004

"I always envy people who smoke and drink and party and don't sleep. Me, I have water and I sleep 12 hours."

Céline, on her love of getting a good night's rest, interview with Irene Taylor, *I Am: Céline Dion*, 2024, directed by Irene Taylor

"The best thing about being famous? Arriving in New York City and asking for eight tickets to see *Lion King* with my son. What's the worst thing about being famous? I can't go because I'm busy."

Céline, on the best and worst parts of being famous, interview with Dave Lackie, *Artists on the Rise*, March 9, 2024

In 2018, Céline contributed the original song "Ashes" to the *Deadpool 2* soundtrack. The powerful ballad plays over the film's spoof of classic James Bond-style opening credits. After the song plays, Céline interacts hilariously with the foul-mouthed superhero:

**Deadpool:** "Céline, that was the most beautiful performance I've ever seen in my life. But we need you to do it again. It was too good. This is *Deadpool 2* not *Titanic*. You're at like an 11; we need to get you down to a five, five and a half tops."

**Céline:** "Listen, this thing only goes to 11, so beat it, Spider Man."

*Deadpool 2*, 2018
Directed by David Leitch. Written by Rhett Reese, Paul Wernick and Ryan Reynolds.

“

Of course, the studio piles up a whole bunch of sort of millennial, friendly type singers that are all incredibly talented, but we just thought, "Let's go right to the legend. Let's see if we can get Céline Dion." So we got a way in through her manager. I sent her a long letter describing what *Deadpool* is and what we're hoping to do, and two hours later she said yes. And then we said, "How about a video?" and she said yes to that, too!

”

Ryan Reynolds, on getting Céline Dion for *Deadpool 2*, *Variety*, May 10, 2018

## July 26, 2024

The day Céline delivered an iconic performance at the Paris Olympics Opening Ceremony – a moving rendition of Édith Piaf's classic "Hymne à l'amour" – from the balcony of the Eiffel Tower!

The performance, her first since her Stiff Person Syndrome diagnosis in 2022, was Céline's triumphant return to the stage and a moment of hope and inspiration for her fans.

For Céline, it was a "dream come true…".

"

My greatest reward is my children. Unless you are a mum you don't know what you're missing or what it even is really. It felt for me that with all my children another heart grew inside of me. Once you're a mum you're a mum for life.

"

Céline, on being a mother, interview with Dan Wootton, *The Sun*, April 20, 2017

"

When you sing 'My Heart Will Go On' in a short dress, it's too much.

"

Céline, on appreciating the over-the-top factor of her hit song "My Heart Will Go On", interview with Sergio Kletnoy, *Cosmopolitan*, November 1, 2013

"It's like somebody is strangling you. It's like somebody is pushing on your larynx."

Céline, on the first symptoms of her Stiff Person Syndrome diagnosis, interview with Hoda Kotb, *Today*, June 12, 2024

> "After years and years of playing hide-and-seek with myself, with my friends, with my family, with my kids. I no longer wanted to be brave. I had tried as long as I could. It was time for me to be smart."

Céline, on finally finding a diagnosis for her symptoms after several years of pain and suffering, interview with Liam Hess, *British Vogue*, May 23, 2024

“When I’m on stage and when I sing a song, what I wear helps me to deliver the song a certain way or another.”

Céline, on the importance of her now iconic designer stage dresses and gowns, interview with Nathalie Atkinson, *The Globe and Mail*, October 9, 2019

"You can't please everyone, so I don't try to."

Céline, on how she operates within the music industry, interview with Elio Iannacci, *Maclean's*, October 27, 2013

“I know where I’m from, I know where I’m going.”

Céline, on her confidence in her career vision,
interview with Larry King, CNN.com,
October 22, 2002

"If I can't run, I'll walk.
If I can't walk, I'll crawl.
I won't stop."

Céline, on returning to the stage to sing to a crowd again, despite her often debilitating health condition, interview with Jayme Poisson, CBC News, June 13, 2024

“

I don’t want to be a queen. I’m the boss. I’m in charge.

”

Céline, on being the boss of her professional and personal life, interview with Elana Fishman, *CR Fashion Book*, August 21, 2019

"Cancer was an incredible challenge for René to go through, and it allowed me to discover strengths that I had never before put into practice. I used to keep everything inside; today I speak up for myself. I pick my own songs. I'll tell a technician that I don't like the way he's lighting me. I've learned to say, 'This works for me... That doesn't... This is unacceptable... This is how I'd like it to be done.' At home I make decisions as a mother, and I communicate my feelings to my husband."

Céline, on René's skin cancer diagnosis in 1999, and how it changed Céline, interview with Naomi Barr, *O (The Oprah Magazine)*, November 2007

“

I was supposed to be here for two months, maybe two years? I don’t know how long I’ve been here now, I don’t count. But it’s a while.

”

Céline, on the unprecedented success of her two long-running Las Vegas residencies between 2003 and 2019, interview with Katie Connor, *Elle*, May 1, 2019

# CHAPTER SIX

# THE SHOW MUST GO ON

For Céline, "the show must go on" isn't just a saying – it's a personal motto and a guiding principle.

She has embodied this philosophy throughout her life, navigating every challenge with grace and resilience. It's also a mindset that has defined her career and inspired her countless fans to face their own struggles with kindness and dignity.

Let's make Céline proud and go out in style. To the show we go!

"

Learn to build your foundations. Figure out your likes and dislikes, and don't ever be afraid to express them. If you can realize you are capable of many things, you'll be able to survive anything life throws at you.

"

Céline, on expressing herself, interview with Naomi Barr, *O (The Oprah Magazine)*, November 2007

“Will I ever sing again? My kids had just lost their dad, are they going to lose their mum? Am I going to die?”

Céline, on the uncertainty surrounding her rare condition – Stiff Person Syndrome, interview with Emma Vardy, *Sunday Times*, July 27, 2024

> “Losing the father of my children, my husband, my manager, the person that I love the most in the world and the person that I can rely upon without questioning anything since I was 12 years old – losing that person was a big deal for me.”

Céline, on losing René, interview with Tom Power, CBC Radio, September 20, 2019

# June 25, 2024

The date the documentary *I Am: Céline Dion* was released. A raw, unflinching and intimate depiction of Céline's battle with Stiff Person Syndrome, the documentary was an outstanding success, leading to the film quickly becoming Prime Video's most watched original documentary ever. It also holds a 100 per cent score on Rotten Tomatoes – a rare feat.

The documentary's success also led to a 33 per cent surge in streams of her music. A standout moment is the harrowing, real-time footage of a severe muscle spasm she experiences, which demonstrates the full, devastating reality of her illness.

"

I've travelled the world many times. And do you believe me if I tell you that even though I travelled the world that I didn't really see anything? Strange, isn't it? It's the price to pay.

"

Céline, on the price of becoming an international superstar, interview with Irene Taylor, *I Am: Céline Dion*, 2024, directed by Irene Taylor

> I try to make the best of myself, to accomplish something every day, to always put the bar as high as I can.

Céline, on how she tries to live a good life, interview with Elana Fishman, *CR Fashion Book*, August 21, 2019

> “When a girl loves her shoes, she always makes them fit. Every time I went to a store and I loved the shoes they said, ‘What size are you, ma’am?’ I said, ‘No, you don’t understand, what size do you have? I’ll make them work, I’ll make them fit.’”

Céline, on her love of shoes, interview with Irene Taylor, *I Am: Céline Dion*, 2024, directed by Irene Taylor

“When you sing it live,
I can’t explain it, other than
it’s magic.”

Céline, on her love of singing live, interview with
Janine Mackie, *Magnifissance*, 2022

"I didn't want people to be tired of seeing me and hearing me. I needed to take a break."

Céline, on taking a two-year hiatus after the worldwide success of "My Heart Will Go On" in 1997, interview with Larry King, CNN.com, October 22, 2002

> "I don't try to be cool, that's not me."

Céline, on being cool, interview with Chrissy Iley, *Women's Weekly*, August 14, 2024

“

I find personally that young artists are selling their soul and it's very unfortunate. When you start in life with selling your soul, what else do you have? What else do you have to offer? It's pathetic and it's very sad for our children. It's very sad for the new generation. I feel sorry for them. It hurts to watch. It hurts.

”

Céline, on the stars of today, interview with Erin O'Sullivan, *Access Hollywood*, September 12, 2013

“I am very spiritual. I believe in myself, I believe in my family, and I’m positive. Through this, you show your children how to deal with things, and how to be strong.”

Céline, on her spirituality as strength, interview with Janine Mackie, *Magnifissance*, 2022

"Communication. It's key for marriage, for children, for everything."

Céline, on her secret to lasting relationships, interview with Erin O'Sullivan, *Access Hollywood*, September 12, 2013

# May 5, 2023

The day Céline's first official feature film debut was released. A rom-com, *Love Again*, starred Priyanka Chopra Jonas, Sam Heughan, and Céline, as herself, portraying a fictionalized version of a global superstar who acts as a love guru for the film's lead.

Céline provided music for the film, and her own real-life love story serves as inspiration for the plot, helping to guide the two protagonists toward each other.

Go check it out!

“Whitney’s been an amazing inspiration for me. I’ve been singing with her my whole career, actually. I wanted to have a career like hers, sing like her, look beautiful like her.”

Céline, on Whitney Houston, interview with Robin Roberts, *Good Morning America*, February 13, 2012

“The fans give me lots of energy. Lots and lots. And being on stage is the gift of show business. It’s like a drug fix.”

Céline, on performing live for her fans, interview with Irene Taylor, *I Am: Céline Dion*, 2024, directed by Irene Taylor

“

Sincerely, I did not expect to win at all! I think it's one of the most beautiful songs, it's a classic. I hope it's going to follow me for the rest of my life.

”

Céline, on winning a Grammy Award, aged 24, for "Beauty and the Beast",* interview with Larry King, CNN.com, October 22, 2002

* The song was a massive success, winning an Academy Award for Best Original Song, a Golden Globe Award for Best Original Song, and two Grammy Awards: Best Pop Performance by a Duo or Group with Vocals, and Best Song Written Specifically for a Motion Picture or Television. It was released as a single on November 25, 1991.

"

I'm one of the artists who sells the most records, and we have sold-out shows. So if *Rolling Stone* say to me that I'm not good, it makes me mad and angry that they think that all of those people who buy my records and come to my show are all stupid, and all wrong. Interview all of them. I can be wrong like this for the rest of my life, and I'll really like it.

"

Céline, on *Rolling Stone*, perhaps the most outspoken critic of the singer, interview with Barbara Walters, ABC News 20/20, September 13, 1999

“My dream is to live in the present. One day at a time. Today, I am a woman, who feels strong and positive about the future. One day at a time.”

Céline, on how she chooses to live her life, interview with Clovis Goux, *Vogue France*, April 22, 2024

“I remember singing for my brother, at his wedding. I sang a couple songs. When I started to feel the love and the warmth of the audience it got me. I said to myself, ‘Really this is what I want to do all my life.’”

Céline, on her first memory of singing, aged five, interview with Larry King, CNN.com, October 22, 2002

"Céline Dion is work work work work work. I have about 675 songs, and I want to sing them all!"

Céline, on her life as a professional performer feeling a lot like work, interview with Katie Connor, *Elle*, May 1, 2019

"It's not how many albums you sell or how much money you make. To have success is not hard. To remain the person that you are is the most difficult thing to accomplish... That's my biggest success."

Céline, on her biggest success, interview with *Billboard* Music Awards 2013, May 19, 2013

“

I sing for the people, because they give me a show every night. They entertain me every night.

”

Céline, on her fans, interview with Larry King, CNN Larry King Weekend, April 7, 2001

"Quebec is a heritage that I give my children and I'm so lucky that I was born here. This is the blood that's going through my veins mixed with some maple syrup. So that's why I'm a sweet girl."

Céline, on Quebec, her hometown, interview with Tom Power, CBC Radio, September 20, 2019

"People thought I was going to finish my career here. And that... the *Titanic* was going to sink again."

Céline, when news broke that she was to have a residency in Las Vegas,* interview with Catherine Thorbecke and Faryn Shiro, *Good Morning America*, April 2, 2019

*Once the place artists go to die, now thanks to Céline's record-breaking residencies, Vegas has become a trendy city for young artists, such as Adele, to have long-running residences.

"I see fashion as an art form, and it's a massively important part of my work, particularly when I'm on stage. Clothes can help you feel strong, romantic or empowered, depending on the song you're interpreting."

Céline, on her love of fashion, interview with Alix Girod, *Elle*, May 24, 2019

“

I want to be remembered as the best mom in the world. I want my kids to always come back when they're married and say, 'Let's go see Grandma.' And I want to cook for all my grandchildren. It has nothing to do with the albums, the money, the awards and how many records I've sold. I'm still on stage because I still love that part of my life, but what I'm most proud of, what I consider my biggest success, is my family – my three beautiful children.

”

Céline, on how she'd like to be remembered, interview with Janine Mackie, *Magniffisance*, 2022

> “It’s selfish to keep wanting more, although I would love a girl. Imagine all the shopping, the jewellery, the shoes, the dresses I could give to her.”

Céline, on wanting a baby girl, interview with *Toronto Sun*, November 12, 2013.

“

I will grieve for the rest of my life.

”

Céline, on the impact on René’s passing, interview with Dan Wootton, *The Sun*, April 20, 2017

“

I hope that the documentary doesn’t frighten people, but awakens people to SPS. It took 17 years for me – please don’t wait that long.

”

Céline, on *I Am: Céline Dion*, the documentary, and the importance of seeking a diagnosis for Stiff Person Syndrome if people experience symptoms, interview with Liam Hess, *British Vogue*, May 23, 2024

"I am discovering myself more and more. Now, I am a woman assuming her own destiny, full of energy and in love with life. It's never too late to start. At 51, I have the sense that I am at my pinnacle!"

Céline, on finding happiness in her fifties, interview with Katie Connor, Elle, May 1, 2019

"I'm convinced that every one of us has a story that's yet to be told, played out, a dream that has never been accomplished, no matter what it may be."

Céline, on life as a story, interview with Alix Girod, *Elle*, May 24, 2019

“

Today is a song that I’ve never sung before. But it’s the most important song I’ll ever sing.

”

Céline, on living in the present, and looking forward to the future, interview with Liam Hess, *British Vogue*, May 23, 2024